# Poetry Collage

*Nells Wasilewski*

First Edition: 2020
Rs. 200/-

Cyberwit.net
HIG 45 Kaushambi Kunj, Kalindipuram
Allahabad - 211011 (U.P.) India
http://www.cyberwit.net
Tel: +(91) 9415091004  +(91) (532) 2552257
E-mail: info@cyberwit.net



Printed at Repro India Limited.

# Dedication:

To my sweet husband, friend, and companion, WK. Thank you for all your patience when I work on my writing and sequester myself behind closed doors.  Thank you for your support and caring.  With all my Love, —Nells

# Contents

# Starting Over

We sold our home
In Harmony City.
Rose bushes blooming,
tomato vines growing—
all left behind.
Neighbors bestowed
snacks on us and well wishes.
A fully packed van moved
farther and farther away
from silence in the car following.
Everything became unfamiliar.
No large maple trees
graced the front lawn.
The house is pretty, larger—
too much space for three.
Empty rooms reverberate
with lonely footsteps.
Days go by:
boxes disappear.
Furniture sits in place.
Closets fill.
Homemade soup simmers
on the new stove.
Inch by agonizing inch
our journey ends at home.

Published Dual Coast Magazine

# Falling in Love

Passion rises and fills
my senses like spring's
sweet-smelling breath.
As I lie in the arms of your
very essence, even then
I long for you.

In early morning dawn,
before sun finds its way to sky;
I think of you
in golden shades of afterglow.

Evening comes and I find myself
falling
into depths
of eyes that shimmer like a hot day
on a long stretch of highway.
I feel as though I am startled
by bright sunlight and cradled
In its warmth.

I forget to breathe, and only, then
realize that I have no need
of anything or anyone but you.

Published in Poetry Quarterly Winter 2018

# Memorable Dinner

I ask him outright:
"Do you love me?"
The only sound was
a breeze rustling
through the open
window, or was it my
heart trying to escape?
I turned away waiting—
When the silence
stretched, I faced him
searching for an answer.
He raised his head,
and gave me his little
boy smile. His eyes
were such a deep blue
I felt as if I would fall
into to their fluidic depths.
He ducked quickly,
but not fast enough!
Suddenly, his strong arms
reached for me and nestled
me in his warmth.
He kissed my lips and
whispered the words.

# Love Lingers in the Attic

Sifting through boxes of
smelly old photographs, and
faded memories add to my
lethargic state.

One picture in particular
grabs my heart and snatches
me from a dark malaise.
Mom and dad stare back at me!
Sixty years spread across
aged faces. Love and respect
written in deep laugh lines

As I embrace this remaining
evidence of what love looks
like, I beseech indifferent
dust motes tumbling through
a streak of golden sunlight:
"Where did he and 1 go wrong?"

# Mine Alone

Enfolded in your arms,
I want to stay.
Encircled in this close embrace,
I feel no need for separateness
or breath.

I need no other solace,
than to rest in willing arms,
and feel the steadfast beat
of your ever-giving heart.

Surrounded in the warmth of you,
the world recedes; time ceases to be.
For the love shining from your eyes,
is mine alone to see.

# Subtle Bonds

Love does not begin
in a single flash.
It grows unexpectedly
in gardens of the heart.
Tiny roots twist and
wind their way into
heedless emotions,
waltz through the land
of cryptic dreams, and
firmly take hold of every
conscious thought.
Suddenly, without warning,
the most skeptical can be
helplessly held
in its fated grip.

# Another Time

If today becomes yesterday,
are all days to be filled yearning
for tomorrow's change that never
comes?

What a shame it is if life gives no
relief from today's sadness , and
only offers consolation of filling
tomorrow with yesterday's
garbage.

Is it better to live in the security
of today because it is more hopeful
than yesterday, or linger in yearning
anticipation for tomorrow—hoping
to efface today and yesterday?

# I Didn't Want to Love You

I didn't want to love you;
what trust I had scorched
and burned away leaving
no embers to flame again.
You refused to hear
or see the tainted side,
so carefully controlled,
locked away and frozen.
Your nimble fingers knew
where to touch the strings
of an out of tune heart.
Strumming gently, you built
up to the crescendo.
Hot words of love swam
through my veins like
a melody, and I melted.

# Spring Storm

Clouds roil.
Thunder, hurling
through the air,
chases sparks
of untamed fire.

Seduced clouds
join a game
of electric
hide and seek.

Wind, snarling like Hades
on a rampage,
impartially
twists everything
in its path

Rain spews
from heaven's
overflowing springs,
enlarges streams
and forces rivers
to abandon
boundaries

Thunder heralds
a farewell salute,
God has spoken, and
a disheveled earth
shakes with relief.

Published in Ruby March 2017

# It's summertime

Sun and fun
lunch by the pool
nap on the chaise
sun-drenched bodies
turning gold
no rushing
no deadlines—

It's summertime!

Getting together
by the lake
loading the
cooler and
taking a break
riding waves
fast moving boats
wind blowing
hair all over—

It's summertime!

Feeding the campfire
making s'mores
telling ghost stories
banking the fire
ready for bed
night sky black,
as a raven's wing,

fills with sparkle
and promise
full moon shines
perfect—

It's summertime!

# Summer Night

Gold-plated day
yields to dusk
an onyx sky fills
with ancient stars
parading
and blinking
in rhythm
with fireflies
Moon's
silvery thread
stitches
moonbeams
across midnight
clothing
earth
in summery
mystique
and the smooth
satin of night

Published by Five Poetry Magazine April 2015

# August in the South

The South is almost
unbearably hot in August.
By six am, the sun
fires down like Hades
on a rampage. Humidity
arrives with its own
brand of misery soak
hair and shirt .
In a bubbly stream beside
the road sun perch swish
in orange afterglow.
Playful neon flashes defy
heat and humidity. I slip off
shoes and pants to join
them.
Peaceful, pellucid water patters across
my sweat-drenched body.
Lazy daydreams cruise
toward brisk Autumn winds.

# Autumn is Here

On the front lawn,
red cheeked apples
beside squashes
dressed in yellow,
compliment
each other in colorful whimsy.
Blonde haystacks,
bright sunshine
pumpkins,
mum's purple bonnets,
and a scarecrow,
make the perfect
portrait.
Orange, red and yellow leaves fall
cuddling trembling trees like babes
in fleecy blankets.
Chill winds herald the season.

# Then Winter Comes

I stand at the portal of change
watching as leaves fall in
scattered silence.
Startling sounds rush
through the deathly quiet.
A wedge of southern-bound
geese betray their purposeful flight
with loud honks of warning.
Bitter winds hiss, a reluctant sun
ducks behind clouds, once
green leaves pool around bare
trees as protective as young
motherhood, and a knowing world
waits with bated breath.

# Fog Frost Splendor

Trees stand still
in frozen elegance,
while ice angels of fog
caress ever-reaching limbs
adorning them in radiant
diamonds.

Morning sun beams
down—through icy limbs
in fourteen carat gold
brilliance tickling
imagination, before
the inevitable meltdown.

Published Poetry Quarterly Winter 2019

# Alone on a Cold Day

I came upon a lone bench
while taking an afternoon
stroll. Loneliness pierced
an empty space deep within.
Maybe it was the frozen
state of solitude that drew me.
The snow-crusted landscape,
with dark ominous clouds
churning like silent freight
train wheels, was quite beautiful.
I shivered and chided myself—
only a fool would be out in this cold
staring at a vacant bench!
I turned to leave, but saw
a sun ray pushing through
pooling in a narrow streak near
the bench. Could that be hope
for Winter's thaw?
When all the snow melts and
earth turns brown again-then
what? Will spring rush in and
save the day?
Maybe, I too will know the
healing warmth of Spring's
caress if it is enough to melt
this frozen core and expose
the true who of me.

# There is always Hope

Though snow may come
and black clouds may hover,
nothing is ever totally
black and white. I know
from experience color
exists even in darkest of winter.
Empty tree limbs and
colorless skies blur my vision.
I strain to focus, dark, dreary days
and fading snow have yielded my
efforts futile.
Searching for Spring
in bitter chill of winter, I see
pushing through a blanket
of crusted snow a solitary cluster
of buttercups lifting their heads
toward the sky full of hope.

# Frozen Fits of Fury

Mother Nature touched
down wrapping the earth
in white with her frosty breath.
Arctic fingertips trimmed
the package with
glittering sequins.
An effortless tirade closed
down the highways,
businesses and schools.
Angry gray skies hovered,
and a collective hush hung
like frozen doom.
Only the children were
able to discern crystal
Cathedrals, sugar coated
cottages shimmering like
precious jewels and streets
paved in brilliant diamonds.
The fourth day a bright
sun bumped the clouds
into motion, and beamed
a ray of hope across a
liquescent paradise.

# Birth of a King

Angels calling
Snowflakes falling
No room in the inn
Mary's time begins

Cattle lowing
Bright star glowing
Strange light fills the skies
Newborn in a manger lies

Gifts are packed
Wise Men riding camelback
Following star to Bethlehem
Falling on knees to worship Him

Unto us a child is born
A king without a crown
Unto us a son is given
He lived to die; we are forgiven.

# Pondering

Impatience grows
waiting for words
to invade head
and heart,
so when put
to paper and pen
they do justice
to the talents
given.

Waiting expectantly
for seeds
scattered in
fertile imagination
to take root
grow and flower
until they present
as lusciously
as cashmere
into beautifully
crafted tributes.

Careful attention
given to birdsong
whispered through
trees in languages
unknown to man,
leaves behind curious

questions as to what
secrets they hold.

Maybe being in
touch with God
is not about
incessant words
but more about
silent prayer—
listening, blooming,
writing or singing
our own song played
out in tune with the Master.

# Restless Yearning

Tossed about
unfulfilled,
I become the wind
flitting here and there.
Something unknown
lures me closer.
Vulnerable, as a lost child
I reach out
desperate.
The Source,
of all my yearning,
cradles me
in His love.
Peace flows
like warm caramel
over ice cream.

# Chosen Path

I walk a path of certainty,
and inhale His aroma
in the earthy smell of salt air.
I am awed by the beauty
around me.
Morning walk beside the sea,
a conch held near my ear
roars with promise of eternity.
I could have walked other paths,
but I chose to follow Him,
and as each day seamlessly
melts into night my soul
is one with God.

# You Called My Name

Lost in a ragged world
of deceit and misplaced
allegiance.

Emptiness, fear
and pain become
combative companions

I know not for what
I search:
A single word
a gesture
a sign of hope?

In mists of darkness,
He calls my name.
A sweet calm
sweeps through me,
as I rest in the presence
of the Great I Am.

# Heavenly Crutch

Some say our God
is just a crutch;
something to lean on
when life proves
too much.
I thank Him daily
because it's true,
what else can His
child do?
For I am weak,
and He is strong;
I need Him night,
and all day long.
I thank you, Lord,
for being the crutch
when this earthly walk
becomes too much.

# Letting Go

Come Holy Spirit!
Bind up the tendrils
of my doubt,
twist them
into braids
of faith

Come Holy Spirit!

Take away the
aches of my
shortcomings, and
heal them with
a Holy band aid of
God's grace.

Come Holy Spirit!

Create in me
a pure heart.
Give me courage
to proclaim
His majesty
and the wisdom
to selflessly step
aside, and let
the Great Yahweh
take control.

# On That Day

On that day,
an agonized cry
came from the cross—
A veil as dark as sin
covered the sun
and cast three crosses
in shadow.
Wind licked
at the bloody body
nailed to the center cross.
Earth shook
until its core erupted.
Rocks burst apart
scattering pieces
of triumph.
The temple curtain ripped
from top to bottom,
granting safe passage
directly to the Father.
Jesus offered up his spirit
the last breath escaped.
Darkness was devoured
by the Light, and salvation
was complete.

Published Ruby Magazine

# By His Wounds

I was the darkness
in agitated clouds
floating in
churning turmoil

I was the splinter
in roughly
hewn wood and
the thorns
in a bloody crown.

I was the nails
that pierced
Your hands, and the
voice that yelled
crucify Him!

I was the sinner
who mocked you,
Yet You bore my pain
and suffering
and remembered
me.

I was the silence
in crowd when you
were punished
for my wickedness.
My well being

fell on you, and
by Your wounds
I am healed.

# Come, Sweet Jesus

Jesus, let me help.
Come and sit with me.
We will talk.
while I cleanse your wounds,
spread ointment and bandage.
Tell me why
you want me to heal your hands.
After I attend the wounds,
we will share a cup of wine.
Tell me your story
while I wash the dust
from your feet.
Come, sweet Jesus,
rest, and I will do my
best to heal
your beautiful hands,
but I so much admire
those holes that saved me.

Published by Ruby Magazine. April 2017

# Shine Your Light

Pitiful, pitiful little tree
standing not as tall as me.

You've boughs of white and bows of blue
with sparkling lights bright and new.

Your counterparts are in the attic to stay
elegant, glamorous and tucked away.

The angel tree and the snowflake with bells
stored with five others in their boxes dwell.

Don't worry little tree and don't look sad—
you honestly don't look all that bad!

Stand straight, little tree, and take a stand.
Shine your light throughout the land.

Light up all four corners of the earth;
proclaim the news of our Savior's birth.

# Don't Leave Me in Savannah

From another era sounds
of groaning and wailing,
fall around me. Loud echoes
of long forgotten pain ring
clearly through the ages.
Singing in cotton fields
reflects misery in rhythm.
Hope being burned out
by a scorching sun.
A young girl of ten and four
too often summoned and
transported to the manor
house upon the hill.
Left in an attic room, but
not alone. Groping hands
reach out; pleas are never
heard. No choices,
no place to run and hide.
Agony and fear filtering
through creepy mosses of time,
cry out in whispered
supplication. Tired defeated
voice pleads, take me far away
from here, but please, please
do not leave me in Savannah!

# Fretful Dove

Mourning dove in a sweet gum tree
sing your somber song to me.
Hollow and lonesome sound of doom,
a rosebud withering before the bloom.

I feel your loneliness deep in my soul
where sadness left a gaping hole.
My heart yearns, begging to be free.
Will despair follow through eternity?

So often dear dove you come my way,
resting on the branches of yesterday.
You're there singing as I gaze and stare,
lost In regrets that left me bare.

I wonder little dove, sitting high above
have you lost someone you can't let go of?
Is your spirit wounded? Does your heart ache?
Is that why you sit there alone at daybreak?

Enduring the agony of each lonely day,
is there joy to be found, living this way?
Oh tell me: on what wisdom do you rely?
What source of strength gets you by?

Where are you this morning, fretful little bird?
I've waited a while, but no song have I heard.
Have you lifted your wings and flown away?
I know you're there but silent, sorrowful and
withdrawn today!

# Discord

We fought
about things
big
and small

Heated quarrels
about
everything
and nothing—

until my head
was full.
I felt it might
disjoint from
my shoulders..

Maybe my thoughts
would scatter
out of Reach
where I could never
retrieve them—

My
emotions threaten
to explode, but
on some level,
I will recognize
a
Blessing
should I receive one.

# Misplaced Union

Passion is gone.
No energy to fight.
Misery has taken center stage.
We used to snuggle,
but now backs turn
detached and silent.
Who was right or wrong
does not matter anymore.
Somewhere between
a wedding day, kids,
stacks of laundry
and a million other things,
marriage was forgotten.
Two cold, empty shells filled
with bitterness and spite
sit at breakfast table,
each feeling alone.
Coffee finished, paper discarded,
a routine kiss on the cheek
and a hasty exit out the door.
I hear the car speed
down the street, in perfect sync
with my galloping heart.
I rush down the hallway,
and retrieve a packed suitcase
from under the bed.

# The Other Side of Rain

Alone in the boat house,
rain tumbles down—
dimples on the lake,
swirl outward like Indecision,
dilating bigger and bigger.
Would it be possible to squeeze
through silvery needles of rain
and reach the other side?

Perhaps the other side
of rain does not exist—
then a place to lounge in sun,
read a book, or misplace the world
may not exist either.
If outrunning rain is possible,
then dare I hope to escape regrets?

Intellect lends credence to truth,
but a stubborn heart holds firm.
Caught in the middle of downpour,
with tears that refuse to fall,
decisions drift out of reach,
and leave me to wonder
where rain ends and tears begin.

Published April 2015 Five Poetry Magazine

# Unspoken Words

Betrayal, lies, hurt, pain,
neatly bound with broken
vows and a wedding ring,
locked in a heavy blanket
of secret pain—

until I saw you today, cocky
and arrogant as ever. An icy
rage raced through my veins
and burst the armor of self-control,
a thousand unspoken words exploded
and hung in the air between us.

We stood there staring,
until the fragrance of freedom—
rose above the surface of pain
and gave me courage
to turn and walk away.

# Damaged

After the first time, he sent roses,
and every time, thereafter.
Over the years, they became
as despicable as a broken rib.

Brilliant, handsome with ready smile,
"Golden Boy" was adored by all,
but she knew the unrelenting fury
of a carefully disguised fiend.

Unsuspected marks of the beast,
in colorful blues and purple lay
painfully hidden beneath
expensive designer clothes.

Lessons were well-learned.
She became less and less visible,
for fear of being swallowed up
in the vortex of his madness.

The last time, his fit of rage
consumed him. She sent roses—
they made a perfect pall.
Everyone came to pay respects.

She stood alone, far out of sight,
cold and detached, watching sleet
destroy the roses.

Published April 2015 Five Poetry Magazine

# Skirmishing with Death

You're there sneaking
around, hiding outside
my door; or lurking
behind the lilac bush
in my garden.

You think I don't know
who you are disguised
in angel wings
tinged with black.
As years went by,
you sat at my table;
and rode in my car.
While keeping vigil,
you invaded my dreams,
and mockingly extended
your hand—

but when I have grown tired
of diminishing breath
and bone, we'll share
a cup of resignation,
and it will be I
who reaches out to you.

Published by Poetry Quarterly winter 2018

# If You Are the One to Tarry

What will you choose
to remember about me?
Will it be the blondness
of hair, or silk white skin
that envelopes
and snuggles close
at night?
Follow our excursion
through the prairie;
stand still among
ancient grasses cavorting
in drunken splendor.
Catch the wind and listen
to the melody of the prairie
whispering sweet words of love.
Look out over rugged terrain
as wild and untamed as me,
for these are the things
you will remember—
when you wander back in time
to a place called you and me.

Published in Harvest of New Millennium 2019

# Final Departure

We watched his essence
disappear within.
Little things forgotten
didn't seem important,
until layers slowly smothered
what had once been open,
vibrant and loving.

Brief moments of lucid
recognition surfaced less
and less. The outer shell
decked out in ordinary
looked the same, but dull eyes
mirrored the vacancy.
Once a single tear glistened
on his weathered cheek;
we chose to believe

that he missed us too.
He existed in unfamiliar fog—
staring and repeating things
many times. Although,
unreachable before the end,
nothing had prepared us for
his final departure.

Published April 2015 Five Poetry Magazine

# If You Look for Me

If you look for me, I will not be in the
usual places.  You will not find me in
the jewelry chest, or the closet that
overflows.  My essence will not linger
in the kitchen with steel
pots and pans,

but if you leaf through poetry books,
you may find me hiding in well-worn pages.
The koi pond with its mellifluous waterfall,
that you so lovingly built, or the flower
garden bursting with myriad colors
may be places to search.

Think of our travels, and take a walk
down a sandy path toward icy waves
falling like prisms of glass against
craggy rock-formations.  Listen to fierce
winds of the Midwest whooshing across
prairie grasses.  Hear me whisper.
Rise high into mountains pregnant
with ancient treasures, and follow the sounds
of a waterfall—you'll find me—inside
the life we shared.

Published by:  Poetry Quarterly – Spring 2014
Ancient Paths Magazine Winter 2015

# Mimosas Along the Way

Outside on the deck,
as far as one's eyes can see,
Mimosa trees hug the banks
of Cumberland River.
Pink blossoms sway
in a frenzied crescendo
of spring, sending out
fragrant signals to soothe
our tattered souls.

We watch barges travel
up and down the river
to places unknown,
saturating calm waters
with mud and silt as they go.

Nothing much to be excited about,
unless cancer sneaks its
ugly head into my camera frame,
and replaces hard won peace with
churning discontent
We too travel an unknown course
muddied and deep as the river.
We become experts
at navigating unexpected
channels, but for a moment
we hide in the beauty
that surrounds us,
pause and take a deep breath

before resuming our upstream
journey in this turbulent
river of life.

# My Brother's Visit

In a dream
of tangled clouds,
I chase you,
running
in and out of sunbeams.
Frightened
and unsure,
I call your name.
You laugh;
hide yourself
in the shadows,
I catch up;
you disappear.
Lingering
on the perimeter
of wakefulness,
I wait, and
hold my breath.
You turn
blow kisses,
and in a flash—
you're gone. Warmth
and joy vanish,
and I am left dangling
on the edge.

Published Poetry Quarterly Fall 2017.

# Piece by Piece

My Dad loses his words,
and leaves in the middle
of conversations.
He goes to war,
or the farm where he grew up.
I follow him there, and we talk
about those things.

He tells of battles he fought,
while holding his imaginary rifle
in perfect military form.
He sees long abandoned gardens
still productive in his mind.
Sometimes
we sit and share moments
over a cup of coffee.
During these brief interludes,
his mind is alert, and we forget
his diminishing awareness.

Piece by piece, he drifts
deep within himself—
his foggy mind closes in.
I want to go with him
and bring him back,
but I can't follow him
there.

Published in Whirlwind Review Spring 2015

# Saving the Last Dance for You

I hear You knocking at the door.
I do not worry about You anymore!
You, with your cunning ways, inviting,
Do You think others find You exciting?

I see your handsome face through the glass,
your smile and charm exudes class.
If I have a change of heart and open the door,
will You sweetly take my hand and waltz me
around the floor?

Will I find myself waltzing down a dark corridor;
losing the battle to my handsome conspirator?
Will You clamp my tired, worn soul with icy grip
and hold me in control until at last I slip?

Oh no, I will fight You with all my strength,
to keep You at arm's length,
until I am ready to give up the fight,
and take that step with You into the night.

Oh Death, I fear it won't be long before I let you in,
and take your outstretched hand when you offer it again.
I'll waltz my last dance with you; my heart will not be sad,
for resting in my Savior s love, I've nothing left to dread.

# So, We Meet Again

A hint of something
hidden, within your still
unmoving smile, stirs
memories best forgotten.
Your silence grates like waves
raking against sandy shores,
evoking emotions I thought
long gone.

My thoughts return to a time
when were young and in love;
we believed we were forever.
The two of us won some battles,
but lost in the end. It seems
death opened its hungry mouth
gobbling up bitterness and pain.
Today the final curtain closed.

And so, I turn to leave you
lying in your new-found peace.
I will swear my tears are
for our children, but they
cascade copiously in rivulets
as clear as crystal not for what
we had, but what we lost.

# Living by the Train Track

A train track runs through our town.
and oh, how I love that sound
of the whistle and the smoke stack
and the clickety clack of the train running down the track.

I smile when I see that familiar smoke blowing stack
Because one day I'll be leaving and I'm never coming' back.
I have big dreams, and I've made a big plan.
One day I'll leave here and become a rich man.

Time goes by so slow in this place! The clock hands never move.
I listen to the tic tic toc, but everyday it's the same old groove.
And then I feel it; my greatest fear,
a decade passes, and I'm still here.

Oh, I love to see the train come around that bend.
It's just like seeing' an old dear friend.
Brings a smile to my face and gives me hope for the day,
when I too can disappear to places far away.

I graduated high school and thought it was time to flee
and shake this town from my heel.
Then my daddy came home and had good news for me,
they were hiring' down at the mill.

I had no money, so I had no choice but to work for a little spell.
I'd have to save my money to buy a ticket on the rail.
You guessed it, the reality of my greatest fear.
A decade passed, and I'm still here.

I can't gripe too much about my life through the years.
Had a wife and two kids and I loved them dearly.
Worked at the Mill and made my way.
Moved up the ladder and had good pay.

Belonged to the church and did my good deeds
I had a right nice house and good friends when in need.
But the yearning' never left to leave and explore.
Another decade passed, but I wasn't counting any more.

The wife passed and the kids moved away.
Woke up one morning and said: "This is the day."
I had one foot up and one foot down,
I took one last look at my small hometown.

I jumped on that train and never looked back.
I smiled when I heard that familiar clickety clack.
A train ran through our town, and I still love that sound.

# Blackberry Wine and Dreams

All was well, who was right
and who wrong
was never an issue
among our elite group.
Agreements to disagree
were reached
and, every
voice was heard.
Cheap blackberry wine
and courageous talk
changing the world.
We would never be
subservient robots—
ours was a mission
to reach toward
the future and fill in
gaps of erosion with
lofty goals and whimsical
reforms.
I didn't expect it to end
like it did—five years were
gone! The empire crumbled,
and philosophical dreams
scattered like debris
on an abandoned beach.

Published in Dual Coast Magazine

# Quiet Dignity

I see the ravaged look
on his face, a grimace
when he thinks I'm not
looking. The pain
writes in red letters
with every movement.
Wobbly knees crackle
like empty water bottles.
A lesser person
might have given up,
and wasted life
wailing about his sorry
fate, but not this man.
With gnarled fingers,
he repairs a faucet leak
with no complaint.
He keeps flowers
blooming, the yard
immaculate, and his battles
fortified with quiet dignity

# Nothing is Forever

You were eight,
and I was seven—
best friends forever.
We reveled in the lie
of perpetuity
giving no thought
to reality.

The magic of fanciful
dreams disappeared
along with the tree house.
Farewells were spoken
with hugs and kisses,
and we were college bound.

Leaning on broken hinges
of childhood promises;
you went your way,
and I went mine.

# Night Song

I sit quietly
in the night,
surrounded
by stillness.
Darkness
has its own reward.
In the distance,
classical guitar music
floats on the summery breeze.
A stranger's voice,
mellow and alluring,
parts the darkness
with a lyrical language,
unknown to me,
and night dissolves
into a slow tempo
of song and infinity.

Published by Poetry Quarterly Winter 2013

# My Mother's Kitchen

When I'm in need of solitude and wish the world away,
I go into a place where I most want to stay...
The smell of homemade cookies permeates the room,
fills me with delight, and dispels all my gloom.

I don't come here too often since that wouldn't be as
special don't you see? But when my heart begins to
wander into this place of memory, I feel her love
so strongly it's just where I want to be.

I walk into the kitchen. I see her tender smile.
I feel her arms enfold me and hold me for a while.
I know that I can tell her all that's in my heart. I
feel a lighter burden as we hug and I depart.

My heart is light; my mood is gay—hard to
turn and walk away. I turn looking for that one
last glance before the door shuts tight. I smile
and leave her standing there as I walk out of sight.

When I'm in need of solitude and wish the world away,
I go into a place where I most want to stay...

# Moonlight and Beach

I bask in moonlit waves
moving like molten silver
crackling and sizzling as tide
ushers toward glistening
sands, and for this moment
in time, I release every
thought, and care from
grasp.
I feel the breeze, hear
ocean's music, and savor
the pungent taste of salt
lingering on my lips.
Quiet hush of darkness
wraps me in sheer silk of night
and permeates my senses.
The only disturbance, white
caplets atop hissing waves.
Feet wander where they
will drawing me deeper
and deeper still into a cozy
cocoon of solitude.
If there is true peace
to be found on this earth; then,
it is seeing God's face In
the magnificence of His
creation.

# With Child

Walking on the beach
dawn skates
smoothly across
the horizon,
leaving behind
a fine shadowy mist.
The sea rises and falls,
its peaceful cadence
out of rhythm
with chaotic thoughts.
I want to efface myself
in the darkest depths
of ancient sea.
I hold on tight
wanting things to remain
the same, but dawn mist
dissolves into day,
and life slips toward change—
as a subtle flutter,
deep within my womb
gives birth to acceptance
and never-changing love.

# Upon Aging

Pain is the crumbling
bones of body and soul.
The mind bids you go,
but achy legs freeze forty
steps into a black hell
of slow motion.

Life is planned in a gullible
vacuum of optimism, as
pride raises its mocking
voice above a yawning
valley of reality.

Today the sun shines;
tightness of joints
lessens. I'll take
a walk, sit on the nearest
bench in the park, and
feed ducks, until the sun
drops low; and forces me
to forge my way home
with burning bursts of
fire that hovers just below
the ability to cope.

Poetry Quarterly Fall 2019

# The Oak of Oak Branch

They felled the old oak tree.
You know the one. It stood
in the town square, shading
old men who sat whittling
odd-shaped masterpieces,
and children who played
hopscotch while their parents
shopped and gossiped.

You remember that tree,
don't you? It was
a monument, a tribute
to the founders of Oak Branch.
It wore centuries of love stories
carved on its face, and held
the town's secrets and
traditions in ancient arms.

The year they cut the tree
the Oak Tree Festival wasn't held.
They waited until the next
year, and renamed it, The New Age
Festival. Hardly anyone came.
Without the oak tree's shady canopy,
the sun beat down like a laser beam
on the town folks setting up booths.

Looking across the empty space
where the old oak tree once stood,

and seeing waning evidence
that it ever stood at all; I grieved
for our beloved tree, and, with great
sadness, grieved the waning evidence
of our era.


Published Whirlwind Review

# Every Heartbeat

The rhythm of a heartbeat,
like an old record, is the same
throughout the years—

dependable, constant, Beautiful.

One scratch on the record
ruins its performance,
as does a blockage to
the heart. Pain gathers and spreads in intensity
as time passes—

growing, gnawing, ever present

Slowly admission rises
above the surface of denial.
I begin to face the truth.
I am caught between
a narcotic haze
and consciousness.
This place is unfamiliar,
too bright, sterile, cold
and buzzing with foreign sounds.
My eyelids feel heavy like elevator doors
sliding open. A stranger
in a mask nods, random
words drift by—

blockage, bypass, surgery

.

I reach out in my semi state
of oblivion searching
for what I so desperately
need. The stark room dissipates
and Mother's kitchen comes
into view, a safe place to regain—

strength, hope, courage

with which to embrace a second chance.

Published by Barefoot Review December 2012

# Father's Masterpiece

Smooth worn
path
caresses my
un-sandaled
feet.
A wispy forsythia
bows
it's yellow bonnet
to pray.
Colorful Cardinals
add a flash of color
to budding trees,
and the lilacs.
Ah, yes, the lilacs!
A whiff of His
fragrance
lingers still...

# From a Beach View

Down below
our balcony,
breaking waves
sparkle
like liquid glass
tickling white sands.
Sun paints copper
fire—
on surfers and sunbathers
living their dreams.
Ocean's
primitive song
mimics
man's soulful cry
for freedom,
and a lone ship,
far out to sea,
travels
a charted course
to places unknown.

Published by Poetry Quarterly. Winter

# At Dawn

From my window,
I watch dawn peep
around night's curtain
creating an entertaining
struggle of day at birth.
Dawn becomes dominant
parting sky in shades
of lacy gray and petal pink.
While Sun 's eager fingers
scrape away
shadows of night,
hope tiptoes across
the sky leaving behind footprints
of inexhaustible
possibilities.

# Layla Lee

You confiscated my heart
child of song and dance.
Waltzing through
transparent ribbons
of imagination,
you held me steadfast
and enthralled.
High spirited, full of energy
and free, you reminded me
of me!
All the things you are,
can and will be
make you every inch the princess
you become in make believe.
It's not your beauty or love
of beautiful things; but, rather,
your delightful gift of love
that enchants, surprises
and captivates.

# A Year to Remember

It was a long time before they told us
to stay home. We didn't know if this
was truth or lies—It happened so suddenly,
and before we knew it, the world
stood still for this pandemic virus.
Businesses closed, work hours were modified,
and medical teams were quarantined in facilities
across all nations.

People everywhere began to prioritize —
checking on neighbors and family,
and actually talking to each other.
The world turned on it's axis as usual,
but tension rose, panic set in
and a rude awakening began.
No antidote to fight this monster
lurking in every corner, while sprinkling
it's deadly germs around like fairy dust.
What were we to do?  Was there light
at the end of this tunnel?

With our idols destroyed, and leisure
stripped away like yesterday,
heads begin to turn toward the heavens.
We pray to the One true God
to walk beside us, as we wade
gingerly through insidious waters
of Covid 19.

# A Better Me

My face is etched
by a trail of years
smooth cheeks
bright blue eyes
gone forever

Visible landscape
always changing
writing my bio
in tired grooves
of elation and regret
deep laugh lines
frame
watery blue eyes
that still know
how to smile

A portrait of former self
on used canvas
faded and crumpled—
a checkered path
charted in twists and turns
that led to a better me.

Published Five Poetry Magazine April 2015

# Southern Belle

I am southern belle
made up of complexities.
Unreadable, impetuous,
frivolous, unpredictable,
I ooze with good manners
and old south charm.
In disagreeable situations,
manners prevail.
I defend the helpless,
cry with the grieving
and pray for the needy.
Make no mistake,
I am spunky and headstrong
with a will of iron.
Oh, and by the way, I like
my tea unsweetened.

Published by Dual Coast Magazine. Summer 2017.

# The Day After 911

The airport's busyness
is at standstill.
No passengers
rush down the halls
to planes or baggage claim.
No smiles or cheerful
greetings.

Spooky inaction hangs
in the air as stifling as
humidity in a rain forest.
People speak in hushed
voices.

Palpable tentacles of menace
envelope nerve-wracking silence.
Tension snaps through hallways;
footsteps echo a funeral dirge.

Outrage, sadness and disbelief
write in capital letters on every
reflective face, while a grieving
nation mourns with unshed tears.

# Whatever Suits You

All I have is a head
full of scattered phrases
and metaphors,

to be spilled across
pages with less depth
than the color of my ink.

Strong stirrings
of summer breezes
let loose to lend
encouragement.

Written down in musical
sketches of imagination
and shared joyfully.
I call it poetry,
you may call it that
or whatever suits you...

*As a special thank you for purchasing my book, I have included a short story for you.  I hope you enjoy reading it as much as I enjoyed writing it*

*—Nells*

# Fever on the Mountain

Living on the mountain was full of surprises, but Beth Benton had never seen snow like this before.  The snowflakes looked like tiny angels winging their way downward, but one glance at the ice forming, on the inside of the window, dispelled any obscure thoughts that heaven could be found on this forsaken mountain.  A rabbit hopped across the lawn leaving tiny holes in the new-fallen snow.  The temperature kept falling throughout the day and so did the snow.  The thought of electrical and phone service failure sent Beth ricocheting back to daydreams of life in the city.

Beth had never wanted to move here, but Jim, being seven years older than she, and quite persuasive, had convinced her. He had grown up in these mountains, and had plans of eventually expanding his logging company.  She had reluctantly agreed to purchase two hundred acres and build a house on it.  At first she had been lonely, but then she got to know some of the women in the town below.  She was especially thankful for Lynn; they had become good friends instantly.  After the children were born, she became a little more content, but she often daydreamed of large department stores and nice restaurants.  She missed her family and formal cocktail parties.  On occasion, she longed for her friends and getting dressed in her fashionable clothes for a girl's night out.  Beth had few occasions here to dress up.  When Jim wasn't around, she would pull out her picture albums and reminisce.

She had met Jim while he was in the city on a business trip, and his good looks had her swooning.  His forceful, almost rough, appearance contrasted with her cultured demeanor.  Jim's large frame loomed over her diminutive one, and filled the room with his presence.  Even though she was petite and quite beautiful, Beth had a special way with her feisty attitude, and she did not suffer from lack of attention.  They were in love after the first date.  Diverting her attention to things of a more immediate nature, Beth came out of her reverie and focused on the storm.

Worry over their situation had Beth thinking about grocery supplies. Jim had said this morning that he could feel the storm coming; he could smell it in the air, but it wasn't supposed to come in for another day or so.  The snow was already falling when he left work, and started home. He didn't waste time stopping at the store; his only concern was getting home.  He didn't want Beth to be up here alone, a thought that made her shiver.  A mental inventory of the pantry and freezer convinced her that they would be alright until the storm blew over.

The kids were spending the night with Jim's sister Lynn and their cousins. Since the road would be closed, they would have to remain there until it reopened.  Storms here could be intense, but they were rarely catastrophic.  Jim and Beth, along with their two children, Benjamin and Ophelia, had weathered storms before.

She went to the window to check on the storm and Jim.  He had gone out to the shed to bring in some wood for the fireplace in case the electricity went out.  The snow had not slowed down any, and she was afraid this one was going to be here for a while.  As Beth was turning from the window she saw the headlights from the pickup coming up the drive. Jim had taken the truck even though the shed was not all that far.  He had wanted to get enough wood to last a day or two in case of electrical failure.

Jim stepped up onto the porch, and she could hear him coughing as he opened the door.  He told her he would see to the wood later, but right now he wanted to warm up and rest a bit.  He came over and gave her a quick kiss on the cheek; it quickly registered with Beth that he was burning up with a fever.  She put on the teakettle to make him a cup of herbal tea.  While she was waiting on the water to heat, she opened the sofa sleeper that was in front of the fireplace just in case.

If the heat went out, they would need to be near the fire for warmth. Just as she finished with the sleeper, the tea kettle began to whistle. Two seconds later the electricity went out. Beth grabbed some of the candles she had put out earlier, and placed them around the kitchen and living room. She made Jim's tea and gave him some meds to take along with it. After taking the medication, he finished his tea and stretched out on the sofa bed. He fell asleep in seconds. Beth stood in the middle of the room bewildered. Starting the fire had always been Jim's responsibility and, quite frankly, she didn't know how to build a fire. The only choice was to bring in the wood, and try until the fire was built. The house was already feeling chilly.

Beth put on warm clothes and rubber boots before heading outside to the truck. The snow was almost up to her knees and still falling. She lowered the tailgate and filled her arms with dry wood. Much to her surprise, Jim had loaded just enough to last one night. Dang, her mind was whirling, and her whole being loathed the mountain with a passion. Her next thought left her breathless and more than a little apprehensive; it was going to be up to her to keep the fire going for days, if she ever got it started.

It was hard walking in that much snow with heavy wood, and Beth was exhausted by the time she got in the house with her burden. She checked Jim's forehead; he felt even warmer than before, and he seemed to be having chills. She piled more blankets on her husband before she went about the task of building the fire.

Beth tried to remember what she had seen Jim do first. She thought he had started with some small sticks, but she didn't have any. She paced around the room trying to think of something that she could use instead. Beth remembered having seen a TV show about making logs out of newspaper, and Sunday's edition was still lying on the kitchen table. By tightly rolling the paper into small rolls, the homemade twigs were soon finished    Beth carefully placed them in the fireplace and she put wood on top of them. It took one matchstick to set the twigs on fire, lighting a roaring flame. She couldn't remember being this hungry before. Canned soup from the pantry smelled heavenly heating up in the iron Dutch oven, as the fire warmed her feet. It was going to take many trips to bring in the necessary wood to keep the fire going all night, self-pity kept repeating, that's his job, over and over.

She put some chicken broth into a cup and brought it over to Jim. With her help, he sipped on it and got almost half of a cup down. He laid his head down, mumbled something incoherent, and fell asleep. Beth didn't know what time it was but she was exhausted too. She ate her soup and took the rest to the kitchen. The clean-up could wait until morning. After banking the fire as best she knew how, she slid under the warm blankets with her husband.

Jim woke her early the next morning tossing and turning. He had pushed the covers off, and he was shivering again. Beth pulled the covers back over him and she laid there basking in the warmth of her blanket cocoon for a minute before rising. When she threw back the covers, she was glad she had slept in her sweats because the room was freezing. The first thing she did was put the remainder of the wood on the fire, and then, she made coffee.

After Beth had her coffee, she pulled on her outside gear and struck out toward the shed for more wood. The next few days were difficult for her; between trips to the shed and taking care of Jim, she made the meals and cleaned up afterwards. She was up many times during the night to give Jim whatever meds she could find and to feed the ceaseless hunger of the fire. It was during one such wakeful moment that she finally gave credence to the resentment growing inside her. She had avoided facing the inevitable long enough. If this storm ever ended and the road ever reopened, she and the kids were leaving this mountain and they were never, never coming back. Jim was welcome to come with them, but if he wouldn't then she was sorry, but she had had enough. Beth didn't think she could go through another ordeal like this one.

It finally stopped snowing, but Jim took a turn for the worse. He woke her up in the middle of the night burning with fever and mumbling. It was too soon to give him more medication so she lay still and prayed that he would feel better soon. She had just fallen back to sleep when he pulled her close and said over and over: "Please, please don't leave me, I need you." He told her many things about himself that night that he had never told her before. He told her how his mom had left him and Lynn to go live with another man. He felt that it was his fault because he had somehow displeased her. In fevered, muttered fragments he told her his whole story and cried. She snuggled close and fell asleep in his arms.

The next morning Jim's fever broke. He drank some coffee and managed to eat a piece of bread. The sun came out and the temperature began to rise. Late in the afternoon, the electric power was back. Jim was feeling better, and his fever was gone, but he was still weak and tired. Beth never mentioned what had happened on the night his fever peaked. She doubted if he would even remember.

Another week passed, and most of the snow was melted. The phone was back in service, and they had both spoken with the children. The road down the mountain had reopened. Jim was taking a nap, and Beth prepared to leave. She didn't wake him as he had been so sick and he needed his rest. She looked around the house and made sure everything was intact before picking up her purse and car keys. She closed the door quietly behind her.

Jim woke up about two hours later; he knew something was wrong before he even sat up. Slowly he got out of bed on wobbly legs and looked out the living room window and just as he suspected, Beth's car was gone. His heart lurched in his chest. It had all been too much for her and he was pretty sure she had found him disgusting hurling all his old wounds and hurts at her. He had known she was lonely and homesick, but he had done nothing to make it easier for her. She had had it rough keeping everything going while he was sick. He should have been the one taking care of her, and not the other way around. Beth was a city girl, and he should have known better than to talk her into coming here. Still too weak to do much else, he walked over to the bed and lay down. He was thinking he would go after her, when he was over this wretched flu, and fell asleep missing her.

Something woke Jim, but an unbearable silence was all he heard. He didn't think he could bear this place without Beth and the kids. He sat up when he heard voices and laughter on the front porch, but before he could get up to check it out, the door burst open. Ophelia and Benjamin ran toward him and started jumping all over him. After hugs and kisses, his eyes focused on the woman standing just inside the door and he actually shook with relief. Beth was standing there smiling at him with a bag of groceries in each arm. When he saw the groceries he knew she wasn't leaving him, and in that instant, he fell in love with her all over again.

"Hi," she said.

"Hi," he replied.

They looked across the distance at each other. Jim was thinking that later he would tell her they could sell this place and go wherever she wanted. Beth was thinking that she would tell him that this was her life, and she could handle anything this mountain threw at her. She had made up her mind—Beth was home and she didn't want to be anywhere else.